A PRAYER

Dan Moses

Foreword

I wrote this book in the form of prayer as a journal between God and me. It was written during a time in my life when I was engaged twice to two orthodox religious girls, with claims to righteousness and clear priorities to be a wife and mother above all else. The first woman had abusive parents who wished her dead, yet she couldn't seem to leave them out of fear of disownment and abandonment. The second girl could never be honest about her desire to be a wife and a mother because that would get in the way of her mother's dream for her to go through school and get a degree. If she failed to pursue that dream, she would also get disowned.

This is happening amongst the Jewish people who would rather profane their daughters to harlotry than marry them off. The Rabbis of the communities fully support the parental actions going against the decrees and ordinances written in the Torah. Typically, they are in fear of losing funding for their institutions or no longer receiving donations from those who have the money. The judges appointed during the time of Moses to help him discern the wisdom to the people were men who despised money. God has commanded us to be fruitful and multiply, fill the earth, subdue it, and set ourselves apart from the other nations. We are a holy and chosen nation, commanded to be holy for God, to create a separation, and not assimilate with the practices of the world. In this book, I pray for us all to submit to God and to educate what that means from the standpoint of a religious Jew whose own nation has been corrupted by the removal of our foundation, the Bible.

The Bible is historical documentation; it is more than a "religion." It is approximately 3500 years old, and 90% of the world in practice believes in that narrative. Jews, Christians, and Muslims all acknowledge and believe that there was a Sinai and a Moses. The Jewish practice requires one to follow the specific commandments listed in the Torah – the Hebrew term for the Bible or Old Testament – and to fully convert their beliefs with the certain actions the book dictates. It narrates one's practice as a Jew to be a priest among the nations and to pass the word of God by word of mouth, from parent to child, when one arises, sits, stands, and rests.

We derive all this from that same document that Moses wrote, and God gave us at Sinai. It is the same unchanged document we call the Bible, Torah, or Chumash. All of them have the same translation in every language. It is a relatively short work. It is the foundation of the beliefs from which morality comes; it is the foundation of all the laws we follow. Most organized Jews don't teach or practice the laws in this book.

It's considered too complex to understand without the leaders of the previous generations who have come up with their own laws, going against the written commandment not to add or subtract. It has only compiled and driven people away from the truth, resulting in 70% intermarriage. Instead, they follow the assimilatory ethos not to marry, date for minimum a year, kill their baby if they God forbid have one, and buy into the lie that their lives will be miserable if they don't go through endless years of schooling or listen to the word of the rabbi.

People's own parents enforce this upon them above things such as love and connection.

For 2000 years, we haven't had our land; we still mourn the loss of the second Temple, which was destroyed for that exact reason. My mission statement is a plea to all Jews and brethren alike to remember your foundation and to read the Torah of Moses, the Bible, and Chumash, and learn truth in a world so void of it.

About the author

Dan Moses is a religious Jew who was raised Orthodox. He's 23 years old and 6 feet 3 inches tall, working as a business manager. He is also a talented artist, musician, boxer, bodybuilder, and athlete of many variations.

Dan was born and raised in Los Angeles, California, where he has lived his whole life. Dan is a twin with five brothers, all of whom were raised by their father, a world-famous actor and a world-class musician.

Along with his entire family, he practices Martial Arts, and has been a tradition in his family, mainly because of his father.

Most of his brothers have one or more black belts. Dan focused on boxing at a high level and has also been involved in other martial arts, but he is mostly an artist. He has worked in his brother's gym under his mentorship for seven years, bodybuilding, nutrition coaching, programming, powerlifting, skiing, and rock climbing, all at advanced levels.

Dan went to an Orthodox school until the 7th grade. He was then homeschooled for two years by his parents. Dan was then shifted to a public charter school and graduated high school two years earlier. He started working as a janitor and a helping hand when he was 16 at his brother's gym. At 19, he enrolled and graduated from N.H.I., a massage therapy school. During this time, he never stopped working and slowly moved up over the years to now manage the business.

His father and mother always made an effort to have him study the Bible/Chumash through all his years of schooling, regardless of all the conflicting ideologies and contradicting statements the "religious institutions" taught. He remained mostly involved with whatever was sent his way, the Los Angeles lifestyle, and whatever else that entails.

When Dan realized that he barely knew where all the laws of his religion came from, he took it upon himself to question the leaders of his community and other communities as well.

He was funded to fly to Uman, Ukraine, where all of the top rabbis and leaders go for the Jewish festivals. He learned that the leaders gather annually to worship a Rabbi's grave.

In the middle of these events, Dan had the good fortune to meet his colleague, friend, and Rabbi, Israel Horowitz.

He had the good fortune to learn the works of the Bible/Chumash together with him, making the same discovery that all the answers are there, and the leaders of the religious/orthodox/ sects of Judaism have been selling a false narrative to advance their own name, not the name of God. Due to this process, he has become knowledgeable and a Rabbi in the truest sense of the word.

Contents

Chapter 1

Thank you, Adonai, my Lord, for blessing me with this gift of life. I know that life is good, and I know the opportunity to be the way I am is a kindness from you. To be born and to be blessed with so many advantages, my kind and benevolent King of kings. To be born a Hebrew, a twin, to have a family who love and care for me, wealth, abundance, and physical vitality.

All this, yet there is a reason to be disappointed. I don't believe I'm ungrateful or that I have a lack of care for myself and others. I have lived my whole life being kind and thoughtful, understanding the most fundamental truth. That God is above all. There is an objective reality on how to live fruitfully and successfully.

I was born with the guidelines to life since I was given the Bible, and it is accessible. Even the most uneducated have the ability to read and write. The day and age in which I live paints the picture of a life that isn't worth working for, and the work that is necessary is slavery. I am not a slave, and my service is not to man. All of man is commanded to work and to guard the field, to be fruitful and multiply, to fill the earth and subdue it. All of us are unique, made with purpose and love. There is no fear of God, there is no shame, and throughout our history, this has all happened before. Resulting in a complete collapse of society. How can I feel comfortable? As if being human isn't uncomfortable enough. Young women have forgotten their purpose. They are taught to start their life, not in the immediate moment, but to push off its start until a more opportune time presents itself. If one is not financially stable, they are unable to pursue love and connection. If they aren't educated enough, women now live in fear of men, even of their own husbands, because that would mean one is reliant on their spouse. If women are highly educated, they lurk over the "love of their lives" with nothing less than I don't need you. Waiting for their men to fall so they can blame them in front of the world.

If one does not have a fear of God, they will put themselves in this position, believing that this is how life is supposed to be lived. How could I not be disappointed? Adonai, my Lordship, you Yourself state, "It is not good for man to be alone. I will make him a helpmate corresponding to him." Women are separating themselves from men, leaving all men with the sort of existence that is not good. Defined by the power above all powers. I am disappointed and disheartened.

I have seen miracles, and I believe in them despite the lack of faith others have. I have been through two very impactful relationships, both of which have been heartbreaking, yet both so necessary. Without this wake-up call, I could not see the turmoil I was in and continued to break free from it. Both women with claims to righteousness that no one except me would or could know about. Families who would rather profane their daughters to harlotry than marry them off to a man who puts God first. Fathers who could never let go of their "little girls" who should be mothers by now, who told me to my face it would be their greatest joy and success in life to be a wife and mother.

I was lied to in grand measure, all in the name of Adonai, the one and only God, the God of the Jewish people. Both women claimed to know I was their husband, as was my claim to them being my wives. I could have seen it no other way, and I asked them to marry me as one should. I was truly in love, and they claimed over and over how much they loved me. It is true they did, yet their ability to love has been broken by their selfish and sick families who want what's best for themselves.

The habits are to lie, to hate oneself no matter the circumstance, and to follow through with their failures till their grave. God has blessed and protected me. I know all comes from Him. During this time, I wrote a prayer, which is a dialogue with Adonai. It came to me as I wrote for the first time, as a journal with no other medium except God. Prayer has been lost just as the present moment. I pray it helps make us submit to God, for He is our only hope in a society so backward. This is what I wrote.

Chapter 2

I walk through the valley of death though I fear no evil, for God is with me. There are truly no words. I lack even the ability to express how I really feel. It's far outside my scope of how to write. I do not know. Help me, please, my Lord the One and only God Hashem. My chest hurts. But what is this really? I need to express the truth - Your truth. It pains me that I live in a world where we do not see ourselves for how we really are. Divine. Perfect. A creation made in the image of God.

I find myself breathing heavily, slowly, and yet it's automatic. I barely understand how I feel, how much less so can I express to the Creator. It all hurts. So much pain. So unnecessary yet also so deserving. Who am I to truly understand? Questions so many questions. Why is it that we are your chosen people, yet we always turn our back to the God, the one and absolute God of my forefathers, Abraham, Isaac, and Jacob? This is no joke. We are so out of line, so out of touch. How can we follow your commandments yet fall so short of what they really are? Your kindness is endless.

We are living in a time of great evil. These evil men, these vile women. I'm truly disgusted. How can I not be? When being okay with it is even worse. I'm stumbling. I know the Torah is important. I can't seem to really get a grip. How can it be achieved? All I do is follow to the best of my ability and know what's on the line.

What is going on? The strangest things I see. How can it all be good for us? I expect to die at a good old age surrounded by the people who made it all worth it. So many believe we are just here. We are not animals. I wish it were recognized that it takes so little attention just to make it work. I see selfishness. This society is based on greed. Why should this not hurt me? Are these not my brothers and sisters? Are they not valid too?

I know I am an individual under God. This gives me power. To break free from childhood and transition into adulthood is not a path most people ever break through. This saddens me. It's hard enough as it is. This does seem to be the reality, though. It is just not an option to be an adult baby, we all know too many of those. Let being that scare you. There's a lot of power just hanging around. Can I handle it? Do I want to handle it?

Please, Hashem, my Lord, lighten these times up with your light. We all need you. Let not your anger flare against me. To ask more based on my past, I know nothing is beyond you. Please, my Lord Adonai, bless me with the ability to do the right thing.

What judge am I? I need your guidance. The whole world does. How can I get away from this feeling? Is the feeling wrong? Do I create these feelings just to create? What does God say?

Faith in God should be all I need. How little I understand about how that works. Why does my faith leave me feeling so aggravated? I feel like I have put in so much. Is now the right time to relax and let it guide me? Why does it hurt this much when I do so? Is this the human condition? What God says about the human condition: it is not good to be alone, from the female counterpart, that is. I can tell you, it is not good. We have been evil since the days of our youth. But there are those who are not. I was good. I am good. I am getting better.

What more am I supposed to do? Can I do more? Absolutely yes. Is doing more the answer? It wouldn't seem so. At this point, I'm plagued by my actions, not the other way around. What now? I don't know. I explore my options and dive into the best scenario at hand with an open mind and curiosity. Many times I have been disappointed. God's guidance is what is needed. I feel like a fool trying to dissect this life. The little I know to be true is constantly undermined. Everyone wants credit, and we do not love our fellow as ourselves just as God intended. I will continue to try, I will continue to fight, and I will always stand for Hashem.

How the fear of death heightens the cost of living. Life is more valuable than death. It isn't predictable. My lack of knowledge of life is truly my biggest doubt. The crushing weight of doubt. Does it truly ever cease? That is death. An inevitable state. If only faith removed my doubts.

As a human, I think we deserve choice, but why are situations made so unclear? Why are my feelings so questionable? Do I not know myself? Do you not know me? My creator, my master in heaven, God of my forefathers, abundant in kindness, and highest of judges. Adonai, please grant me peace. May I feel your presence around me always, may I never doubt in you, and may you make me a more righteous man. It shames me to ask for the thought that arises, can there really be enough to give back? Who are we to deserve such kindness?

Please do not conflate my wishes with the wicked sinners of the past, and please accept me, for you know what is in my heart and mouth. I am bound to you, Hashem, my Lord. I wish to know you more, that I may be humbled to have such an opportunity and that you forgive me for my iniquitous ways as I stand before you, as I am. You are my judge, my Lord, the truest opinion. Please redeem us all, show us your face, and do not continue to turn. We all need you more than ever, the world, your Jewish people, and all that live within it.

Don't we all need confirmation? Accepting that need is good. Where we get that need met is where it gets tricky. One should always seek confirmation from God. Modern man seeks validation from society since they are all too weak to individualize with God. The modern woman seeks attention. Mainly the attention of weak men whom they can control. Which nowadays gives women a lot of power. I cannot believe I live in such a time that we wouldn't notice the God-given differences between man and woman. This society has killed their own sexuality to pursue their undesirable fantasy.

Stay positive. This feels like the religion of today. It would be nice, though it's not relatable or possible, given these strange circumstances. Chicks with dicks, money worship, abominable relationships, and a desexualized society. The list goes on. Why is sickness relatable? Again just another idol. This society I live in is so void of God. People don't know what they are. We need truth, not more sophisticated opinions. It would seem the most relatable aspect of the modern day is this void that we feel.

"Well, if you follow the statistics, we are happier than ever!" I've seen enough. I cannot continue to pretend this world isn't corrupted and misled. Hold on to what you know, it may be all you have left. Let your individuality shine and create contrast everywhere you go. This has nothing to do with proving yourself to others. Be honest to yourself and never lie.

Whether a life is long or short, it is God's judgment, and He is most merciful. We cannot see why, trust God's judgment. There is a reason, and it is always a kindness. I wish to have a long life, and I want to make it. I follow His commandments in the hope I have security. I pray every day to feel it. Even with this slippery feeling, my faith grows stronger and more powerful. I pray this world holds on to God and His commandments. If only we treated our neighbors as ourselves. How much better would we treat our wives, children, and ourselves?

A family is a unit. Together we are always stronger. Not all units are strong, and most units bring each other down. We need to fall into place and acknowledge the blessings we have and mourn for our sins. This is the way forward. I wish to achieve a family of my own. I'm confident we will be powerful, loving, and protected. The spirit of God will guide this family. He will guide me.

This is no small task, and it cannot be achieved alone. "It is not good for man to be alone." Please, Hashem, raise me from this void and make it clear to me the actions I should take, for I am lost without your guidance. I do not bow to the gods of others. You are always at my forefront, and my desire is to be closer to you.

O master in heaven, how easy it all is with your guidance, what a better existence we'd have. Nothing could feel better in our relationships with one another, women, and families. We all need to open ourselves up to the obvious fact that we have been created. Please, Hashem, heal us speedily in our days. What humanity has done with this "choice" is beyond belief.

How could we be given so much yet use it all so ill? The righteous that follow you with their hearts and their mouths may their blessings stand out. May these individuals feel all Your goodness. Hashem, I pray that I am counted among your righteous, for how could any of us get by without your help?

The existence people doom themselves to is not short of all the descriptions of hell. The levels of suffering in this life always shock me. It's all too hellish to bear. There is more after this life, and it seems to be correlated to one's actions and where they end up. This is true for this life as well. If you feel yourself falling short, yet your actions are righteous, expand your frame. How can this help me? What am I supposed to be doing? Should I be doing something else? My own mind processes with action. I need to broaden my mind. There is much on this earth untouched and hidden in plain sight. My sacrifices should be done with words, may it be a pleasing aroma.

How little I remind myself that I am being watched? My creator infinitely above, infinite in all conceivable ways and past. I need to hold onto this. If the skies would rip open to reveal, there is the most infinite being on His throne, beyond the heavens, beyond the universe. Gazing down on me as a speck. Yet only that would be a small aspect of God. For Him to look upon me scares me.

What am I to be deserving of this? If I am capable, what would you have me do? I pray to you, my Lord, that you not become angry with me, for me to ask how? It still seems necessary to ask even with the knowledge of your Torah. Your loved one Moses, he asked. I feel the fear, yet I do not know you. It is still my deepest desire too. Please, Hashem/Elohim, may the process be glorious and blessed. May it be your will that the whole world open themselves to you, and may you bless us all with your glory.

We need to let go of this image. Our own physical image. Glorious it may be, but such a small fraction of glory and the glory Hashem allows us to have. I am so much more. Can I get to the point where I live in the first person? Is it what God wants from me? Or is it my disgust with the vanity of society? Moses was the prince of Egypt. He broke free. May your Torah continue to guide us all. Please give me the strength to have people who support this journey so I can make it to the point where your spirit rests heavily on me, and I see you.

Count your blessings. The prophet Ezekiel for all his worth was given an upgrade from human feces to animal feces for food. I cannot thank you enough for all my blessings, Hashem/Elohim. The best parts of life are when we function on instinct. It guides us with no try at all, and yet the experiences are so full. I pray to maintain that for my life, knowing it is God who guides. The male-female dynamic is lost. It is our fullest state of existence. Do not lose it. It is going to take the help of everyone and anyone who would rather not hide in the failures of their parents and accept a new fate for themselves.

There is much to say about feelings. I know exactly how I feel until I start to feel guilty for feeling "it." Let "it" go if you follow God. If not, keep fighting and don't stop. Never stop until the guilt is gone. We are all experiencing "it." "It" can be defined. "It" is your doubt, stopping you from feeling good about things you should be feeling good for. We are all creatures made in the image of God. We are built with purpose, yet most choose death. Adam and Eve did. Correct the original sin. Change yourself for good. In the pursuit of righteousness, "it" is all worth "it."

Hashem/Elohim, I feel so honored to be heard. You have always been watching, and you are always listening. Your abundant kindness is so beyond my comprehension. The little I know, you allow me to know. I will continue to express the truth and your Torah always. It scares me. Please, Hashem, my Lord, benefactor in heaven and all around. Please make it a pleasant journey. The change that I continue to go through may it be a glorious change. Help me let go of my fears and doubts. Help me help the world and fulfill my purpose as a chosen one of God. I speak and write to you to help me never fall. I do not wish my fate to be the same as others in the past. I do not wish to accept certain "realities." What I know to be reality is you, Hashem/Elohim nothing is beyond you.

As I write more, the feelings overwhelm me. There is so much conviction yet so little certainty. This state of being does not seem to be unique to me. We are in control of nothing. I don't wish to be given control at risk of my desires taking over. I wish for you, Hashem/Elohim to take control. There are no better hands. This is not the reality I live in. If you are allowing me to take control, please bless my desires to be holy and pure. With the Torah as if it were a part of me. The work ahead looks undoable. Make me see the path, remove my silly ideas and replace them with good ones. Who am I to complicate the simple? For it is all outside my ability to define. Engrave your truth in me.

These were the first pages I ever wrote.

When I finished writing this, I met the second girl in my relationship. She was right out of a fairy tale, and she told me everything I needed to hear. She didn't really want anything that she told me, and her loving mother couldn't bear to let her go. The details are unnecessary. During the period of time we dated, I sobered up to who I am and always need to be.

According to the modern parent, without a college degree, your life will only be depressing, and the less important things, such as love and marriage, can wait. I didn't have time to wait. I definitely shouldn't wait for someone who doesn't want to marry me from the moment she knew me. Don't fall into that trap; you'll marry a bitter woman, and she will make your life a living hell. King Solomon says there is nothing worse than a contentious female. I think the wisdom of King Solomon is valid. Wisdom is at Adonai's command; fear Him and follow His commandments all of your days.

Chapter 3

Thank you, Hashem/Elohim, for all my blessings. My life is dedicated to you, yet you give this life to me. Your kindness is overwhelming. You have answered my prayers, and you have made me ready to receive them. There could be no other time, for I was not the man I needed to be. This journey ahead seems long, but now it seems more achievable. You have granted me additional relief. I continue to open myself up every day in order to accept the truth of life. This life is a grand gift given to us by the source of life itself.

Everything is in its proper time. I try to expedite the process, only getting closer the more I try. The change is rapid. Accepting my position for being as it is has freed me. I accept how you have made me perfect as I am, with no comparisons to others. We are all unique. We need love and confirmation that it is all okay. We can receive this from one another, understanding who we are. I am a man, and this world was made for me.

I have a woman made for me. We can, and we will correct the original sin. This itself is a lifelong journey most people fail. Remove the comparisons. The reason to love one another is far more compelling than your desire for knowledge. Once you know, there is no turning back. Most would rather stick with the "choice" than admit their own mistakes. God forgives; there is no one like Him. If only we understood the gap.

"Please, Hashem, show me, your majesty, that I may be better and more humble every day. Continue to guide and shape me into who you need me to be, your humble servant"
-Dan

I have seen a vision of some kind. It seems to be a riddle. I've processed it to the point in which it is always God who leads. I've been blessed to arrive at a point of true freedom. There is only one of me. I don't want someone else's experience. Give your life credit. Never doubt your own ability to share. "It" is who we are.

Remove all ill will against yourself before you can move on. All of humanity is rapidly changing. Can we accept that about ourselves? Every minute, every hour, every day, there is a new change. This should always be how it is. Accept fully and move on to the next stage in life. There are many more.

What could be more desirable than the right way? If you had the least bit of courage, you'd take up the rod. Most never get through life, even with God. No. It has never happened. If only people knew these grave mistakes. It goes so deep. The leaders have misguided everyone. They do it. Why? Money, power, fame, greed, sex, self-loathing, and for approval. There are many combinations of these. "They" and "them" do this to you for these things. How can you buy it? I don't know, and I'm happy I don't. Be simple with God. You know in your heart and in your mouth. I know in mine, and I pray that the whole world is enlightened. It could only be achieved by Hashem/Elohim Himself, our most benevolent. Until then, I humbly await your arrival. Your servant - *Dan.*

I need to feel it, and it needs to be worth it. I am of flesh, yet I am much more. Mind, body, and soul. That is a much fuller and necessary existence. My mind needs to be stimulated, my body needs pleasure, and my spirit is me. When I achieve this, I'll know I'm ready to progress. I know there is a state of oneness, I wish to be whole again. There is such a state of familiarity, yet it feels so strange to be reunited. It is the state of going down the path of oneness.

I need help, and the help needs to be given without hesitation or annoyance. This needs to be a great joy. A joy felt so deep within one understands it as their purpose given to them by God. How little I know the effect of my words? I pray they land and affect everyone for good. May it please, my Lord Hashem/Elohim.

I am a man pursuing my destiny. I know it is one given to me by God. I must not doubt the truth as being too much to handle.

How can I apply these rules to myself, yet it does not relate to others? If God says it is good, it is good for all of us. The truth cannot push those away who are seeking it. Trust the good in people and ask God to guide your tongue. There is nothing beyond Hashem. He loves those who fear Him and follow His commandments. Do not be selfish. Act for the sake of the last line of good men and women left on this earth. Do not let the guilt of disappointing man skew your judgment. I worship one God, for He is the One and only God, Hashem/Elohim.

Adonai, my God, it is true. You have taken us from the depths of Egypt to the land you promised our forefathers. Hashem, my Lord, I know your words are true; I do not rely on the word of man. I love You with all I possess. I pray it is enough. Your loving servant David, he followed your commandments, and he bled for you. His Psalms are beautiful, and he has far more ability than I. Please do not forget that I have bled too. Please shame my enemies. Smash them as you have always smashed the wicked. I am not a man of great ability such as my forefathers, and your beloved. But I wish to be loved.

I wish to be recognized by you and for you to help me overcome the burdens. I cannot understand the lack of feelings or the void I feel. Please show yourself to me and help this world. For it is not within the ability of man to do so. We are so far gone. I pray I am not too far gone. Raise me up, my Lord Elohim, to walk with you my whole life and never disappoint. May the foundations I refuse to let go spread to the world and create a heaven on earth as you have intended. Build me up, my Lord Elohim.

May the commandments flow within me, and may the mockers be demolished. Save me from the burdens of the unworthy and strengthen me to know the difference. Fill my soul with your spirit and cleanse me every day. Blessed be the righteous, and cursed be the wicked. You are the truest judge. I tremble before you, and you only. May I feel the blessings in all the necessary ways and give me the understanding to know what I need. I love you with all of my being, your servant - *Dan.*

Hashem, my Lord, most high in status. There is none like you. I bow to none other, and my fear is a fear of disappointing you. I live my days trying to maximize my experience. When I walk for you and speak of you everywhere I go, you bless me with the divine experience. My faith in you determines my days. May it continue to grow each and every day until the day I lay to rest. I am free, and I am at peace with myself, though I strive to be better every day. You grant me wisdom and ability, though I know myself as a simpleton. May your light shine through me, giving others faith in you. May you allow me to help as an instrument for you, most holy one. Fill my spirit with your attributes. May your enemies hide in shame. Please, my Lord, lift us all up so that we may live.

This life is not how you intended it. It is void of your Torah. We have lost the basics, and yet the wicked and lost preach the word of man. Remove the wicked and enlighten the lost. How can we see without your light shining in the dark?

Heal us, my Lord, for there is no other who can. Do not destroy us; listen to my prayers and know my heart is pure. You have cleansed me, your kindness is so overwhelming. You forgive the iniquities of all of us. I pray for the good of mankind, for the sake of your Torah, for this is the message. I will fight for truthful justice, life, kindness, love, and the pursuit of your commandments. Help me help others so that they can help themselves. May we use it all for good. Amen.

I fear you like no feeling or power on this earth. You have forgiven me, my Lord Elohim, and that confirms you to be more kind than words can express. I am speechless, so I write. For the truth of the righteous has your shine. Who else can we discuss with and be understood? Who else guided us in times of need?

None other than you, my Lord, most high in status, most holy. No matter who comes my way trying to bring me down, they cannot, for you are with me. The futility of life creates a need for redemption, and there is no one who can save us but you. I bow to your glory and splendor. Please accept my offerings of words, for I am but dust. I cry to you in faith, for my blessings all come from you.

Praise be He, Hashem, my Lord Elohim. The necessary feats of life give us the feelings we need. This everlasting journey does not last. You give us so much. Please do not turn from me on my request. I wish for it all to brighten the day and to see your majesty in all your works, of this existence and beyond. May the pain not be too much to bear. Please release us from this pain. You have deemed it so treacherous. May your words shake the world and connect us all. I know, like no other words, that you are "Adonai, my God, it is true." Remember the Shema prayer. Remember your foundation. For without it, there can be no righteousness. Only futility. Save us speedily in our days, for we await your arrival, Hashem/Elohim. I love you with all my heart and soul, your servant - *Dan.*

I give thanks to you, my Lord, for all the circumstances in this life. Praise be He, Hashem/Elohim, for it is you who places me where I am. You continue to bless and protect me, as promised in your book of the Torah. This world I am born into comes together in unity to work against you.

They are but dust to the wind, powerless against your command. You privilege the righteous with your guidance in the direction of beauty and life. Where the wicked work against themselves. How little power we have, ones only hope is to turn to you, my Lord Elohim.

My Lord Elohim, your kindness is so overwhelming. You grant requests beyond one's wildest dreams, and you put them into one's life when they have the ability to receive them. Your kindness is praised upon the places of most high and holy. I will always sing and praise your name, selah! The good you grant man has been in front of us since the beginning. Even alone and in the dark, the only light we can hold onto is our knowledge of your kindness and mercy, my Lord Hashem/Elohim.

You have given us life from the dust of this earth and the whole world with it. How the wicked blame you for their transgressions. O, how I tremble in fear of angering you, my Lord. For your ability knows no bounds. You have connected me, my Lord, a kindness that knows no limits. May I always have the strength and courage to stand for truthful justice and the pursuit of kindness. In a world whose foundation is resentment of this gift of life, how can one's response not be anger? For we all know in our hearts and in our souls that there is but one God, Hashem.

Hashem, how wonderful is your work! I myself am a creation by your hand. You protect me, for I am no fool to think it is I who protect myself. I give myself over to you freely as a man humbled by your blessings. I observed tonight that we all have so much to give and so much to offer one another. If only this world would humble itself enough to give back to the eternal giver.

We are all lost without you, and those who give back, even if just to others, you bless them, for we are all your children. We connect when we understand ourselves.

This is how we can help one another and find you within. Most have tried to remove you and have succeeded in crushing themselves. We are born from dust, and we return to it.

I pray to you, my Lord Elohim, that if there is a way to redeem us all, please tell us so we may stop all this futility and truly feel. Humanity, your children, have chosen to avoid this gift of life rather than achieve fulfillment through you. There is no feeling that is better than this. How can I rest knowing I am so incomplete? I always turn to you, my Lord, for there is nowhere else to go. Forgive me, for I had turned to other places when I was in doubt, not utilizing the full truth. I have so much to learn, yet how can that be the road to heaven on earth? It is you, my God Adonai, the one and only who can allow it. So I came back to you, my Lord, seeking truth to fill my soul. For it is not me who is the judge, but you and only you, Adonai my God. May it be your will Hashem, that the truth is revealed to us all.

Shabbat has ended, and now the week starts. Day one is the beginning. Creation. The cycle repeats, and we repeat with faith. "Adonai, it is true." This is the end of the Shema we repeat twice daily. Why? Because God said so. Fear of God is more real than anything man can ever say. There is no exception to the rule. We know it is true. More true than truth itself!

Our foundation is lost. We preach ourselves, not our God. The righteous are lost. That is not who you see who fills these positions. Your god is not my God. He is Adonai, Hashem/Elohim, my Lord and benefactor, teacher of all that I know. The One and only God. Stop preaching against the attributes of Hashem, our God. See Him in His book. Use it to see in your life, for we are blind! All we see is what is in others' lives. "Life is a movie?!" Who are you, and what are you doing? This is our life, given to us, and this is our Torah by God's merciful kindness.

Our foundation is simple. Read the book, follow the commandments, and serve your God. "Who do you think you are!" I'm the one who's "considered" insane for saying words like that. I talk in praise of my Lord, knowing my differences, and accepting myself for who God made me. This has never been easy. It is worth every minute and every second. Thank you, Hashem, my God, for this gift of life.

This life is beautiful. The great beauty of this universe is given to us. Hashem, my Lord, your kindness knows no bounds. You withdrew from the darkness in order to create. We are all given the opportunity to create. We have to remove our evil and make room for you, Hashem, to dwell in us.

You hear our prayers, my master in heaven. We ask you to know the difference between right and wrong, so we can make a choice to do good. If only we had taken notice of the answer to our prayers. Your divine attributes of mercy, kindness, and a slowness to anger are definitions we know. We claim to agree you are all this and infinitely more, yet we cannot apply these attributes to one another. I pray You forgive us all, for it is a great shame to be so foolish.

Our fear is misplaced. The orienteer of life and death has always been you, my Lord Elohim. For my fear lies in angering or disappointing you and no other. Nothing can happen to me if you don't allow it, for your judgment is always fair and just. I learn from the experiences you give me, for everything is connected. We all come back to a single source. It is you, Adonai, my master in heaven, my King of kings. Enlighten and save us all, for it is not until you command it that we will return to you, blessed beyond our wildest dreams.

My desire in this life is to walk with you, Hashem, my Lord Elohim. Your kindness is so overwhelming. You have granted me the blueprints for all your chosen nation to do so. How could I be ashamed of this desire? Your commandments truly elevate us past our physical self in order for us to be in your likeness. I know I must start there. I am, but a worm, slowly crawling across a universe of infinity. Nothing is beyond you, my Lord. Please expedite the process for us all, for this is the only way.

I will not give up. There is no choice. I crawl slowly, but it is you who will grant me wings. I await transition, excited for all the change. Blessed be He, who cleanses all iniquities, my Lord and creator Hashem.

You have made me a man to work and to guard your garden. But I live in no garden. I pray to you, Hashem, creator of all, that you let me into your garden. I know the sins of my forefathers, and I do not wish to repeat them. For my desire is to listen to you and never partake of the fruit of the tree. Place me in your field so I can fulfill as you desire for me. So I may be fruitful and multiply, fill the earth and subdue it; and rule over the fish of the sea, and the birds of the sky, and everything that moves on earth.

"False is charm, and vain is beauty."

A righteous woman should be the pursuit of all young men and all men. Not only will she make you great, but you will also see greatness in the form of a woman, and she will be fulfilled through your achievements. This is unity, and that is the full picture. If you are not a righteous man, you cannot receive a righteous woman unless she chooses you. For all women, if this is your choice. Bear it and show the world you are capable of changing the path of a wicked or lesser man. Do not let your perception deceive you of the choice you made.

We remember and follow all the commandments of Adonai so that you will not stray after your heart and after your eyes, after which you want to turn. Do not let your desires over which your eyes delight ever let you forget who you are and where you come from. If ever you do, never doubt the ability of Hashem's kindness to forgive. Do not be like Cain. There is sin so terrible you cannot return, for God will turn His face.

"Surely, if you improve yourself, you will be forgiven. But if you do not improve, sin rests at the door. Its desire is toward you, yet you can conquer it." All the guidance is in the Torah, "be strong and courageous, and I shall be with you." Hashem, my Lord, I crumble at your majesty there could be no other truth to follow. I will obey and follow with all of my heart and soul, your servant - *Dan.*

The power of words. It is in your mouth and your heart. Your heart holds all meaning. Your mouth needs to be heard by God. He is watching you, and He is so kind. He gives you the ability to act. This is the only way to prove to Hashem, your Lord, that you love Him and devote yourself to His ways. Please, Hashem, destroy the wicked and evil men and women who use your name against you. Your justice is always just, and your reasoning is only revealed if you will it for man to see.

Forgive me, my Lord Elohim, for I am but a child. I do not know how to forgive myself, but it is not I who forgives. Your forgiveness is unspoken among your chosen nation. My Lordship, I remove myself from this perversion, and I set the difference for your glory everywhere I go. Please, Hashem, my Lord, bless me with courage and strength so that I may always follow your will.

This life I live is not how you, Hashem intended us to live. Forgive us, my Lord, for it is upon our own actions which we continue to live this way. Do not punish the righteous with the sins of their parents. Show us your face so we may not see our evil. Better to die righteous than to die anyway. For this life, we stand here to correct is the life of our inevitable death. I wish to walk in your garden in only the ways you intended for me, for I did not eat of the tree of death.

Thank you, Hashem, my Lord Elohim, for always protecting me and teaching me through the placement of the day. The truth connects all, for it is objectivity. All our experiences play out differently. If only we understood our differences, could we appreciate one another? The heart of man is evil since the days of his youth. I will not allow the wicked to slander your name, Hashem, my Lord. Grant me the strength and courage which is necessary to be truly righteous. Do not allow the world to continue in its ways. Show us your face and eliminate this evil with your right hand.

Everything which I know to be true does not line up with everyone else's narrative. I have come to the discovery that your truth Hashem is lost. It will always be true, but men would rather follow their narrative. They control so little yet hold on to being their own creator. Enlighten us all, my Lord, for the consequences will be what they will be. It is why we seek your redemption. This life was intended to be good. Please bless us all so we may know it to be true.

We are all your children, for we come from you. My father in heaven, may my acts and the actions of the righteous of this world calm your anger and allow you to show us your face. So we may all live in harmony and unity knowing our place in this world, so you can grant us access to the next.

O, Hashem, my Lord, redeem us, please; it is not a matter of waiting. How can this suffering go on? Your children are sick, heal us and stop this plague of the mind. My brothers and sisters truly matter. I am of the same lineage. You, Hashem/Elohim are our father. How could it be unfair? I know you are the truest and most high of all. How can my judgment be right? I fear stepping out of line, for my fear of you is so grand. I do not wish to give doubt for the things you show me, Hashem. You have shown me that your children are truly suffering. So greatly at that. It is the sort of suffering only you can bring upon man for going against your commandments. "Judge with truthful justice." Is it not true that if we fall from your commandments and ordinances, we are crushed? My own life has been blessed beyond what I considered achievable only for listening to and applying your commandments.

Another truth of yours, Adonai, "not by bread alone does man live, rather by everything that emanates from the mouth of God does man live." We all have the ability to hear you, and most choose to block their ears. What else can I do other than pursue your commandments, acknowledge my position, and repeat your words? I will continue to do so all my days, for my desire is to walk with you, and I will not feel shame or guilt like the wicked for wanting a position so fulfilling it almost removes my choice. Your kindness knows no limits, for you love those who serve you and follow your decrees. Praise be He Hashem/Elohim for all of eternity. Amen.

We are blessed with so much harmony, and I don't believe we need all this chaos. Keeping it in the loop allows the chaos to affect your life. There are so many complications in life. Stop allowing the chaos to affect you. Surely you can improve yourself. No wonder the bar is so low. It does affect others; stop being so selfish. Please, Hashem, my Lord Elohim, forgive us all for our transgressions.

Truth is being spoken, the righteous are willing to preach the truth with no shame. I do feel the internal conflict. I was not always a righteous man the way I am today. You, Hashem, have forgiven me. I know how kind, gracious, compassionate, and slow to anger you are, my Lord Elohim.

I repeat with no shame, for I do not wish for my actions to be limited by others' limited ways. There is order. You have given it to your chosen nation. The rest of the world does not have access. The access I have is because of you. Your love for us all is a kindness beyond our wildest limitations. You define the good in your book of the Torah, Hashem, my God. I will continue to follow, knowing this great gift of life is given. You do this for the love of my forefathers, who have done the actions which you need to repeat. I pray we acknowledge what we've been through. That you forgive us all, and we see you clearer in all that we do. Bless me, my Lord, and bless all my brothers and sisters to lift the suffering off of us all. Amen - *Dan.*

Chapter 4

Why, Hashem, my Lord, do we experience all this conflict? I know I am seen by you, Hashem, for you are the only comfort I receive. You are so kind. Humanity has lost touch with its divinity. How could you not be the clearest value that this world has to offer? This life was given to us by you, yet our minds are in other places and things. Serving you, Hashem is the smallest of prices to pay for this life, for the more I live, the more I see there is no cost.

Life itself without the deepest desire to serve you, Hashem, is worthless. Just a bunch of worthless meat-bags who hold on to "our" way. I know you, Hashem, my Lord and benefactor in heaven as my God. A God who gave us "good" and has been the only giver of blessing. Heal me, Hashem, for you love those who serve you with all their heart and soul. I follow your commandments even if the necessary feelings are not present. For who am I to disagree with the word of God? I will not pretend that I don't understand your Torah. It is clear, and those who claim otherwise do not read it.

How could my strength be used against me in service of you? Do not let my tormentors stand. Make them realize their mistakes. May they be redeemed through truth spreading through your undeniable spirit. May it be your will, Adonai, my God, that you make the path clear for us all, and if anyone chooses the path of the wicked, destroy them to dust. Praise be He Hashem/Elohim, God of unparalleled kindness, mercy, forgiveness, beauty, harmony, slowness to anger, and truthful justice for all of eternity.

Amen!

There is so little acknowledgment of others when one gets lost in their own picture. The grandest frame includes all of us. Please, Hashem, forgive us for losing sight of the truth. Treat your neighbor as yourself. There could be no better words to live by. That includes everyone you meet.

Today Hashem, my Lord Elohim, I found myself to be greatly stressed. For everywhere I go, people would rather not collaborate with your Torah at risk of money, control, greed, selfishness, and much more. I identify these attributes specifically, for it is among the most that I see. There is a constant struggle of identity in these times. There could be much relief to that pain if we acknowledge you, Adonai. Only then would we know ourselves. We could let go of this false sense of control and live in heaven. I pray to you, Hashem, to free us from this exile. I cry out to you, Hashem, for who else listens and who else can handle the state of the world but you? I do not feel like part of this world, for it has become so corrupted. Yet I find myself unable to escape. Free me from this perversion and bless me and those who set the difference. Let the world know by example that you can only be redeemed one way. Adonai's merciful kindness and willingness to forgive those who love Him and follow His ways. I pray we all acknowledge the need for harmonious collaboration, the willingness to help and guide one another to a life that fulfills the mind, body, and spirit. Shine your light upon us all, Hashem/Elohim, for we need you more than ever. Amen.

The feelings that flow through me are not being mirrored, for men and women do not care. We all have voices, yet we're afraid to use them out of fear of being yelled at!

Not by you, Hashem, does man fear, but by the empty threats of man. The sort of upkeep it takes to get through the day is so obviously cosmic. Everything is connected, for our source is you, Hashem. Can I live this life feeling the necessary feelings?

Why, Hashem, do I not feel appreciated by others as I do by you? Are we disconnected enough that our soul no longer communicates or needs nourishment? From you alone, Hashem, do I live, not from man and their wicked ways. This world prioritizes goals and responsibilities for the workplace, not amongst their homes, wives, brothers, sisters, and children. How could one lose sight of the necessity of love? I love you, Hashem, my Lord, for my love for you makes me better. The acknowledgment of how little I know directs my feelings and faith to you, Hashem. Heal me, Hashem, for my belief that people are better than they get credit for has let me down so much.

I always encourage others to feel welcomed and recognized, yet the response I get is a spit in the face or a tiresome redirect for another time. We do not have time! If we are so blessed to live a long life, it is Hashem who allows it, and it will ultimately feel like the blink of an eye. Hashem controls life and death. For the angel of death sits on the edge of every action. Be better and improve yourself, for Hashem, our God, will forgive you. If not, your desire will consume you.

Praise Hashem, our Lord, and creator, who answers all our prayers. You test us, Adonai, my God. You do it for our benefit, for you love us. Hashem, my master in heaven, I understand now more why it is you built me through these tough and harsh experiences. I would either make it or die. You couldn't be there fully, for this wicked world does not deserve your attention. Blessed be He Hashem/Elohim, who does not turn his face from the righteous. It is you, Adonai, who has kept me alive and has won my battles for me. Without you, I would end up crushed without the desire to live.

Praise be your name for all of eternity, selah! It is only He who gives. I wish to give back to you, Hashem, to serve as you requested. To fulfill your commandments and follow your ordinances. Blessed be He, my kind God Hashem/Elohim, for, through your kindness, you bless us with all that is good in life.

I will talk to you and praise you, Hashem, when I walk, sit, stand, and retire. We all need to earn your light, and you have blessed me with the guidance of your Torah. I seek wisdom and knowledge of you, Hashem, my Lord. For it is you who makes the simpleton magnificent. May it be your will, Adonai, that you bless those who love and fear you with the comfort that their servitude to you is recognized, with a shower of blessing beyond the dreaming capacity. You, Hashem, have no limits. Show us your grace and mercy. Pull us from this exile and protect our children for the sake of your name. Praise Hashem for all of eternity. Amen.

All of the upkeep for the sake of servitude to Hashem, my Lord Elohim, is never overlooked. People wonder why their life is not blessed? As I look around, I see wicked people who live with no fear of God. There are a few extraordinary and wise men who know that, at the very worst, chastisement from Hashem is like a rebuke from a father who loves a child. The basis of our relationship with our creator is founded on love. The struggles we all go through can be solved through the willingness to bring out the best in oneself in order to bring out the best of another. May our love and praise for you, Hashem, grant us redemption in these times of great evil.

There is no price for truth, only reward. Lead with truth in all your endeavors, for it will not let you down. Hashem is so kind and benevolent, He has granted us His Torah. It is the root of all success, wisdom, safety, and fulfillment that one can have in this life. It is also the source of truth, so read it carefully and acknowledge the reward that comes with it.

Hashem, so kind and great, slow to anger, and cleanser of iniquities. Grant me wisdom and discipline to follow your Torah, to bind it to the template of my soul so I may shine as the righteous do and receive the blessings to which you shower those whom you love. Destroy the wicked who claim your name and act with duplicity. May it be your will Adonai that you uplift the righteous to be like your high angels. Whom you give orders to destroy the evil that exists in man and woman. To cleanse us all that we may return to you for all of eternity. Amen. The week has come to an end. I am approaching Shabbat, and my work won't be complete until I recognize what I've done. Each and every week, we mirror creation, seeing the fruits of our work. If we do not apply the discipline that is requested, how laughable are we in the eyes of God? Hashem's creation and His days are so much more than we can imagine. In the end, it was good, and he rested. Thank you, Hashem/Elohim, for bestowing your kindness upon us and giving us rest in our lives. Without the end, there is no beginning.

I have learned this week that the capacity of some has been limited because they do not acknowledge God's endless ability. You, Hashem, made us, in your likeness, a piece of infinity. We need to start with the basics. If only man had fear of God, we could all collaborate and make one another great. Having no worries about the extraneous details we cannot control, for we are but ants among our God, though even ants work together to build a home. Please, Hashem, forgive us, for we are foolish.

Bless us with wisdom so that we may see. I pray your children don't let their evil outweigh their good. I know it is you, Adonai, who deals truthful justice, condemning and serving what one deserves. Men have turned work into business, and women have turned help into control. I, your servant Dan, work for you and only you. Fulfilling your every wish. Bearing the rebuke I receive in order to be holy for you, as you have intended for me to be. May it be your will Adonai, that you grant me wisdom and protect my heart. All that I do is in service of you.

Praise be He, Hashem, my Lord Elohim. It is from you where we come from. Your kindness grants us many blessings. I cannot pretend that serving you, Hashem is not my greatest joy. Your children, my brothers, and sisters look at me with great disdain. They do not follow you, for they are in fear of talking about you. The leaders are responsible for taking the innocent minds of children and tampering with God's Torah. Destroy them from this earth, Hashem, my Lord, cleanse this filth from our midst so you may dwell in us all.

Hashem, it is you who grants wisdom to those who are willing to open their eyes. This world wasn't built with anything less than perfection. "It was very good."

Man was good, but the creations of man's heart have been evil since the days of our youth. The breath of life was blown into our nostrils. God's creations are perfect, and it is what man chooses to do with life that is evil. Bind your heart to God. Make the right choice, for the fate of humanity, is in your hands.

We are all cosmically connected. Do not doubt your actions to be any less than judged. We are servants of Adonai, Hashem, God of my forefathers Abraham, Isaac, and Jacob. These men are not God. They are flawed men who have corrected their sins. May we all be the same. Amen.

Whatever Hashem's commands will come to be. Continue the correct actions, and don't doubt your intention to be any less than good. Hashem, you know my every thought. All of me is in service to you, and there could be no turning back. My burning desire is to follow your commandments, to prove to this world that all comes from you, Hashem/Elohim. You have granted me my own story unparalleled by anyone else.

I accept the position I am in fully. I walk with the divinity of Hashem, for I am holy for Him. Hashem is not happy. Men and women covet what is not theirs. They sell themselves for harlotry freely and commit adultery. Hashem's anger burns, and I feel it in me. It is much to bear, please Hashem, my Lord. Tell your servants what it is we can be doing to calm your anger so you do not destroy us.

I am ashamed to exist amongst the perversion. May the light which you let dwell in the righteous burn the evil to dust. How is it that we do not rush to serve you at every opportunity we get? Send me more opportunities, for I serve you and only you, Hashem, my God. I know in my heart and soul that if I pass your tests, you will bless me beyond my wildest dreams, for you are a loving God, so kind and gracious, slow to anger and just. May my words appeal to you as a guilt offering for even being in the midst of such perversion. I will always stand for you and shine for the sake of your name. Amen.

Hashem, my Lord, I cannot rest. I cannot continue to stand as a bystander to this great evil and worship other gods. Grant me the strength and ability to crush them, for I know my safety lies with you. Guide my tongue to be sharp and wise. Revealing the truth of the Torah to all who ask. May the truth of your Torah give those who seek you the ability to act against the current of evil.

How could it be that I live in a time where fathers and mothers don't want their children to marry? The child and the virgin cease to exist. Only those who are truly righteous can withhold themselves for you, Hashem. Bless the children and young girls to have protection against these evil parents. Give us all the courage and wisdom to act as we are, for there is no better time than now.

The fear of underdelivering for things we don't have kills our ability to have anything at all. Do not doubt

Hashem's ability to uplift those who serve Him. Dive into the belly of the beast, for this is the road to redemption. Accept that with Hashem, all your battles are won, and you can succeed. The failures of those who did not have faith do not affect those who serve Hashem. He will provide for you as He always has, and He will save you as He has from Egypt.

Praise be He Adonai/Elohim, my master, my creator, my deepest love. The more I know you, the more I understand myself. In the likeness of the unique one. I am unique. You have granted me the wisdom to understand but a small fraction of myself, which is all gifted to me from you, Hashem/Elohim. I love you with all of my heart and soul, and I will follow blindly, for your greatness is above all else. I question you for answers, not in doubt of you, my Lord.

Love is not a selfish act. It is wholeheartedly giving without question. We remind ourselves to love our God with all of our hearts and all of our souls. When you give, you get. There is no such thing as something for nothing. Be wise where you place your love, for we are limited only in the likeness of Hashem/Elohim.

"Love your fellow as yourself." The foundation which allows you to be like Hashem is love. His kindness is limitless, and He grants us guidance, for He loves us. You cannot receive love unless you give it. Serve Hashem/Elohim, master of legions, for your lacking only comes from you.

Nowadays, love is a term for movies. A fruitless undesirable, sexless term for infatuation. If you can break free from the desires of your eyes and heart and say the truth always, Hashem/Elohim will love you all your days, and you can walk with Him for all of eternity.

Hashem/Elohim, I will never stop my belief in you. My faith in you is tied to my soul, which I am blessed to still have. This world I live in is Godless, so void of soul. No matter the issues I face in my life. I know that you, Elohim are with me, for I fear you above all else. There could be no situation that could deter my heart, and I pray for the path ahead to be blessed.

How can I worry knowing I hold on to the truth of your Torah? Despite the harshest of tests, my forefathers passed them with only delight in their hearts to serve you, Adonai. Life itself is in your hands only, for the heart of the King is like water in the hand of God. I discipline myself to ground myself in the necessary work of service to the master of legions, creator so divine, one and only Adonai or Elohim. Please, Hashem, protect me from the evil who live to hurt the righteous. Destroy them, may their requests of destruction fall on themselves.

Bless me, Adonai/Elohim, that I escape this evil, have the necessary tools to combat the wicked, and be part of the change that the world needs. Only your holy spirit can allow such change to create a cosmic shift for the good of mankind. I will continue my pursuit of fulfilling your commandments with uprightness of heart, alacrity, and speed.

Bless my actions to be undeniable and for all men to bow before you. Blessed be He for all of eternity. Amen.

Adonai/Elohim, you have given me peace of mind, and you have calmed my soul. How could I not see your hand in everything? I remember my prayer, and you grant them all. How could one forget that everything is in the hand of God? I see my progression and how far you've allowed me to come. The journey has just begun.

I know in my heart that Hashem has rewarded me in this life and the next. To become a man in these times requires the strength of the good. I am a man, made in the likeness of Elohim. My purpose is to work the land, to fill the earth and subdue it. All action that I take upon myself is for my benefit, for those who serve God know that He, Adonai loves those who serve Him. Be cautious with the actions you choose, for they determine your life. Only with the kindness and mercy of Hashem/Elohim can one arise from any depth. I am but a pebble of sand against the universe. I am not the ruler. Adonai/Elohim is. Grasp the task at hand, for if you do not, sin rests at the door. Do not let your ego dwell in you, for the spirit of Hashem cannot dwell in such stupidity. Let go of your false sense of control, live the life God intended for you and do the right thing. Hashem's requests are simple, and the best things in life are too. Allow Hashem, your Lord, to bless you and save your soul from the requests of man. Amen.

Chapter 5

Adonai, my savior, you lift me up from any struggle. How can I be conscious of the right thing yet struggle at the same time? I can be better and purer. I pray for you to guide me on the path to overcoming my desires and never second guess in the face of truth. I know nothing, yet I know enough. The only way to keep anyone and anything in place is to understand your position under God. Do not boast about your position, be in fear of losing the position you're in. For a king will not reward the boastful servant.

The one who performs with joy and happiness is loved. Start with your parents, your siblings, and the people around you. Show Hashem/Elohim that you put Him first and listen to His ways with your actions. Trust in Him to reward you for your stillness in times when it is necessary. For what more could one do other than act their desires out if they open their loud mouths?

Guard my tongue from evil and improper speech. May it be your will, Adonai, that you make me a more righteous man, one who walks with you all of his days and for all of eternity. There is nothing other than that desire that can truly ever last. I hear the iniquitous screams of the wicked who try to bring me down. Please, Hashem/Elohim, do not allow them to affect my mind. The way of the people around me is not your way. Give me strength to always follow you and quiet the screams of desire.

Amen.

All comes from Adonai, my God. Work hard, fear Him and follow His commandments. The reward will come to those who do, not to the lazy. Do not let your desires overtake you, see the fuller picture, and what is important, that is what you should pursue. Each day I am allowed to see more. The beauty of Hashem's creations is beyond the ability of words. The week comes to an end, Shabbat is near, and I am blessed to rest.

The struggles men and women deal with are vastly different. Do not let the snake near; stomp his head and scream with disdain. Work together, use your strength, and warn one another of the conceivable threats to unity. Know that if your foundation is Torah and truth, your words cannot be flawed.

Humble yourself, we do not know how small we are. It can all be over in an instant. You do not know what tomorrow holds. Take today by the reins. Show your Lord Adonai what you will do with His gifts and opportunities He grants you. Change yourself, for everyone else will just bring you down. Grow strong and know that it is not forever.

Adonai/Elohim is communicating with us. Listen well and open your eyes. You should strive to be like the heroes of the Torah, not ashamed of thinking you are capable. Adonai will bless you at the right time. Act ready every day, for it will happen if you pass the tests. Show Adonai, your God, that you recognize what He has done for us and act for the sake of His name. Amen.

Fear Adonai, your God, for only then can you lose fear of the how. This earth yields to man all of its fruits and all it has to give. The commandments of Adonai/Elohim. When it is our time, we will go. If my God wills it, I will not see tomorrow, and there is no one who can stop it. You must pass the tests and have no worry about what will come, for it will end up better than you imagined. Be strong and very courageous. Only then will everything come to you.

"And Noah found favor in God's eyes." If it is necessary, be the only man and woman to set the difference. Do not follow the gods of others, cursing yourself with a fury of casualness from Elohim. Fear will take on a new face if you can truly comprehend those words. Death is part of life, and there are fates worse than death. Choose life, love Adonai, your God, and do not be casual with His requests. If you consider yourself worthy, be ready for a real test. Not a test from school, a piece of paper made for the human zoo that dictates your success in life. A test made for you and only you.

One that knows your deepest insecurities, fears, and worries. It will come down to a simple yes or no. Do I love Adonai/Elohim enough to experience any loss and still fear Him more than that fate? Choose yes, for if you do, Adonai will remove your worry and fear for life. He will shower you with blessings that only the worthy deserve, and it will last forever.

If faced with the truth, there will be many who join the true service of Adonai/Elohim. The truth has been lost, and the Torah is a parable in the eyes of man. Remind yourself of the events that have happened. Remember your exile. There is no escape from work. Shabbat is our only rest. Creation is good. Strive each week for your work to be very good.

Do not live your life with the fear of loss, have fear only of Hashem and lead with love. It can only be seen in action, so serve with all your heart and soul. Hashem, our God, is kind, do not mistake your under-delivery for His lack of ability to recognize.

You are seen, and you are judged. Reprimand your fellow as yourself. Rebuke is served to those Adonai loves, from a father who loves His son.

The challenges we have to overcome are fundamentally the same. Woman should have enmity with the snake, and if she does not, she is willfully evil. Do not be deceived. She will make you partake, and now there is no going back. Both of you have introduced death to your life. It is the job of all men to stomp the head of the snake, and if you are bitten, so be it.

Hashem will heal you and reward you for it. For the righteous woman who yells for her husband's help, she is loved by Adonai. She understands her position, and she will always see the fruits of her work. It is all work. Shabbat is over, and you are thrown back in. Let's see what you can do. Adonai, guide us and bless us all. Amen.

It is only through your hand Adonai that we live. You allow us to see a small aspect of your judgment. But it is not enough for us to claim we know. I know nothing, Adonai, forgive me for my lack of understanding and enlighten me of my mistakes.

I walk with fear of you. The more I walk around, the more my eyes are disgusted. The lack of shame I see comes from the wicked soul. My fear of you, Elohim, makes me tremble. I am afraid of the fate of those who do not serve you and judge incorrectly. I wish not to judge but to be surrounded by those who accept your rebuke and are blessed. I am so afraid, my Lord, I wish to serve you, and I doubt my own ability to serve. I am willing to throw myself in fully so that I can learn from your command. Please do not let your anger flare. I wish to please you and serve you for all of eternity. I am a human, a man, flawed and imperfect. I will strive to be perfect for you, for with you, I do not need to learn by failure. Bless me, Adonai, my God, with the ability to serve you and reap the fruits of my hands.

I do not know what it is that I have done wrong. Please tell me so I can correct my sin. My heart aches, and my soul cries, for I know I am not yet fully accepted.

Please strengthen me to pass the test, and may I live to see the majesty of your blessing. Amen.

My heart aches, and my soul grows tired. Lift me up, Adonai, my master, the state of the world is Godless. I'm so confused. How could it be that we have your Torah and the resources to understand, yet man places his action in service of himself? It is necessary to escape. My soul is at threat from all the impurity. You do not wish to dwell in this perversion.

Do not turn from me, my Lord, all of your children have been victims to great lies. Children who grow up are victims of the failures of their parents, who torture their youth with their insecurities. Men and women torment themselves with their own weddings and feel guilty for not unifying through a materialistic medium. Children hear the lies of their parents and the lies of society and need to choose a lesser evil. The truth is hidden in an infinite pool of "knowledge," and only the "few" who can consume it have all the answers.

For the few men and women who love you, Adonai, they have no choice but to be a wandering spirit navigating against the current of sin. I know your judgment is flawless, and it is I who does not understand. Please enlighten me with the answers I need and allow me to live a life filled with your Torah. I have found the Torah, no one wishes to follow you, and no one believes me. I pray that those who do are blessed beyond and that I myself feel the confirmation of your blessings all my days.

Adonai/Elohim, forgive me. I assume I know. In truth, I do not, and I wish not to anger you. It is You who has created the sun, moon, stars, the earth, and everything in it. Your power has no limitations. I am in fear of making false judgments, for your judgment is perfect and righteous. I am but a man, created and impure. What I know, you allow me to know, and I pray for your council all my days. I await your command and to hear you. Even if it is in the form of rebuke, I will beg for your mercy and forgiveness.

Please tell me what it is I am supposed to do. I am in pursuit of your commandments, yet there is a collaboration that is necessary to progress. I believe you are preparing me for the right time. I do have doubts, and they are not in you, my Lord, but in my own ability to do the right thing. How can I pretend I know? It is why I need to be spoken to by you, Elohim. I am afraid, but I am willing to take any leap if it comes from you.

I remember my exile in Egypt. You saved us with a strong hand. You led us to a land flowing with milk and honey and guided us with miracles all along the way. The judges and kings have fallen. The prophets have suffered, and I wish to be anew. I have the most beautiful opportunity to know their mistakes and see the reward for their struggles. I do not wish to glorify the past. It seems very much a repetition in a different light. But there is no light, only darkness, and I tremble in fear of your destruction. Do not destroy us, my Lord. Reveal to us the necessary truth. Only then will we be saved.

Who are we? How complicated we make the simple. It shows how little we know. We are dust, and to dust, we will return. Be silent, let Adonai teach you His wisdom, and allow your fellow to be acknowledged. We do not know God's reasoning. Accept His evident truth and follow it until the task is complete. Your faith needs to be strong enough to accept death if ever in opposition to His commandments, and you must understand it is just. What you want is usually what works against you, be more concerned with what you need. Hashem's reward is better than your reward. Open yourself up to receive such awesome gifts. Be confrontational. Battle your evil within, and do not worry about what others think, for they are not even listening. If they are, give them the opportunity to engage. We exist among each other under the one and only God, Adonai. How can you not defend the very miracle of your life? The submission to man, which exists, only continues from our lack of care for our fellow in support of the grand futility.

If you do not fight for the freedom of others, you will lose your own. God granted all of us unique abilities, a piece of infinity in service of the infinite. Adonai/Elohim, I will not bow down to the idols around me nor assimilate with the disgrace. Death is all man's fate. Better to die now than to feel the burning wrath of Adonai/Elohim for denouncing His name. He will save you, do not rely on a man or any angel. For it is Adonai who saves our souls.

Adonai, my Lord, I pray for your enlightenment. How can I know what it all means? It is you that commands understanding. It feels so much like all the struggle can be avoided. It is you who will bring an end to all the suffering. When we collaborate together to apply the teaching of your Torah, that light shuts out all this darkness. So few are courageous enough to speak and act. If you are righteous, you will arise again and see the end of days. All the futility will continue until Adonai brings it to an end. People are awaiting their death as opposed to rushing to life, which is not an everlasting opportunity. Your actions have been acknowledged. Adonai sees all. Be on the side of the righteous, acquire wisdom and command better of yourself. If you do not, you will be consumed by sin, engulfed by your desires, and waiting for your death. Recognize that it is not you who commands wisdom.

Adonai/Elohim, my King of kings, molder of universes, we are but clay in the hands of its molder. Forgive us for not rushing to serve you and for our denial of how we are made. All we can do on this earth is acknowledge you, tremble in fear of disobeying you, and pour our love for you, Adonai, into everything we do. Shabbat is near, and your overwhelming kindness allows my soul to rest.

I pray you judge my work as good and guide me into the next stage of life as you always have so that I may shine like the stars forever and ever. Only with fear of God and following His commandments can this be achieved. Throw yourself into the flames of the furnace, for Adonai will show you it is a summer breeze when your faith aligns with Him.

Adonai, may we praise your name for all of eternity. Amen! If we use our ears and listen to you, all of mankind will be saved. Fear God, follow His commandments, and love Him with all your heart and soul. This is for our benefit. Your glory and majesty are so beyond our human comprehension. May your children glorify you all their days. You have allowed me to reach the unreachable and to see your hand molding me into the man you grant me access to.

My desire is to fulfill your commandments and to rely on your kindness as the best possible alternative. You chose us as your beloved nation, fulfilling your promise to my forefathers. I wish to be holy for you as you requested, for it is my greatest joy. Blessed be He Adonai/Elohim, who grants blessing and plants the seeds for all blessings to grow!

Chapter 6

Your kindness is overwhelming. I never stopped believing, and I never stopped praying. Now it is I who cannot believe. The way in which everything comes together is far outside of a simple task such as belief. When it does come, the satisfaction you allow us to have only comes from your divine hand. All comes from you, and there is only one God, Adonai/Elohim. My actions have been seen, and they have been given encouragement. I cry tears of joy, for my work has seen abundant fruits, and it all comes from you. Thank you, Hashem, for all that you do for us and all that you have done for me. This life is good, and I see the truth of your Torah in everything.

Blessed be He Adonai/Elohim, who commands the start of the week. It is you, my Lord, who sets the stage for all. Thrown back in, in order to complete the divine tasks. You are so good and kind. Without your guidance, we are lost. We are betrothed to you, Hashem, my Lord. It is forever. You sanctify us, Adonai, and you permit us access to your blessings. Bless those who serve you with confirmation of their actions that are aligned with your will.

No matter the difficulty, no matter the doubt, no matter the laziness. Remember your covenant with Adonai, His awesome miracles, and His voice at Sinai.

These events shaped the new world to be good and created a contrast to the darkness. Choose life and have no worries that any other option is better. You will only strip yourself of the present moment and the ability to have a future filled with life.

If you truly fear God, love Him, and follow His commandments, you will live like the days of the heaven on this earth. No other gift could be worthy of your attention. See yourself as that man. One who wants the gifts that are better than any palpable thing on this earth. Your higher self is a piece of the King of kings.

Be like Him. In His likeness, you were made, and I have been told to be holy for Him. Adonai loves us all, and His wishes only allow us to see Him more. I pray I see you more every day, and I fulfill my destiny, pleasing you with every blessing and every struggle I overcome. May this new week be blessed with love, unity, joy, and the spirit of Adonai. Amen!

Adonai, I am at a loss, and I need your help. I cannot get through the day without it, and there would be no days without you. You are the source of all. I remain curious. Could it be I am more concerned about what I think I need as opposed to what you have in store for me? Forgive me, my Lordship. If this is the case, I will stop at nothing to correct this.

What troubles me is that there are realities at play that you clearly present in your Torah, yet I cannot see how childish I am. "Surely you can improve yourself. Otherwise, sin rests at the door." Forgive me again, my Lord, for I believe it is I who must improve. Surely I can, and I will try again until I see your countenance.

How can I pretend, and why do I even try to solve these riddles? My head throbs and I feel nothing. This can't be good. I am in fear of eating from the forbidden tree, a return to this false idea of being alone. You are with me, and it is you who gives me women. It is you who saved me from the fate of man. It is You who has guided me up until this point. Please, My Lord, tell me what I must do in order to correct my sins.

To be purer, to be ready, and to be who you want me to be. I'd be willing to do it all over again if it were what you wished of me. I pray to you to reveal to me what is necessary and to forgive me for my lack of awareness. I have made a proclamation for you. I pray it was the right one. I did not make a vow. I pray you show me soon. Amen.

The necessity for courage commands us to better ourselves and to fight away the great threats at hand. Adonai, bless me with bravery and strength to implement the truth. I know that you will save me. You will show me your plan. I pray I do not sabotage myself with lesser actions. I let go entirely, floating to the top. I began to fully relax. It is you, my Lord Elohim, who raises me up, and shows me kindness and truth. I will not encourage false beliefs. I know only the words of your Torah to be true, and everything else has been proven false.

I will not go to the right or to the left of your command. I will not add or subtract. You grant us broad access to which to achieve success, but your requests are clear. The way to achieve clarity is only through Adonai and His commandments. All things good come from the creator and so much more. It is not I who defines good.

I am merely granted access to such goodness. We all are, and He allows us to pick it up wherever we go. I pray we all snatch up the opportunity lying around us and have the courage to combat the forces working against us. It is only possible with your merciful guidance Adonai, and you are my God. I will serve you for all of eternity. Amen.

Adonai, your mercy is so abundant. You save us from the clutches of death. You are the provider of all, and your will is carried out without delay. What you have in store for me is much better than I imagined. I know I will always choose you. There is no judgment other than yours.

You have asked me to not eat the forbidden tree. The knowledge of good and evil. It is not for man, for anyone who takes of it brings death into life. The source of your Torah is life itself. It is purposeful and filled with blessings. A grand gift for man to have the opportunity to correct the incorrect. We are born into this life pure.

This purity needs to be held through life. Do not assume your path is destined to be impure. You bring it upon yourself with your false promises in the name of God. Man is given Woman. She is Hashem's gift to man. God notices man's unfulfillment without his helper. It already feels like too much to bear. Man's ever-changing and ever-expanding character only shows his divinity. We are all in the likeness of Adonai. Women can decide not to partake of the forbidden tree. She can be divine as well, do not ever put a righteous man in the position to join you with your sin.

Do not eat, for she will whisper in your ear, "I know God better than Himself, trust me, was I not created for you to help you?"

Walk away. God will bless you with the reward of all the fruits and a woman so good she will make other women look like animals. She will support God's will with no adding or subtracting. Redemption can take us right now. Have you had enough? Are you happy with yourself? Is it all too hard?

Are you being mistreated? All I hear are excuses. We all know what's coming, and you will only be redeemed if you are righteous. Enough everyone with your wicked ways. You have to develop the ability to say a firm NO. Be careful. The police will get you!! Be extremely careful, for God will get you.

They push perversion upon people who believe they need to break free from the "lies." It's a false premise, and you can only break false premises with the truth. Try to say it no matter the doubt and no matter the fear. Command better of yourself and protect the vessel which takes you there. I feel the coming up of Rosh Hashanah already. It can all change at the last moment.

For the good or the bad, we know what it is, and we are here to correct that mistake, so another as bad does not arise. There is nothing above God. He is the master of all. Be so privileged to serve under His way, not the way of resentment and your own ability to act. I will not compromise with truth. Let my testament stand before you, my Lord Elohim. I will not have good proclamations be used against me, and only truth can stop me. Adonai, truth is in the palm of your hand. Bestow it upon us for all of eternity. Amen.

Almost time to rest. Shabbat is here. Stop working. Move fast, since you don't have time. You need to rush, and you need to run. God gives you time, and He gives you death. You already know good and bad. We are correcting this condition. You can live like the days of heaven over this earth. Love Adonai, for he loves you. Let His countenance bless you all your years. Do good and know this. You know nothing. Humble yourself to your Lord, our Master in heaven, all your days.

Enjoy your rest. You work for Adonai. You are His servant, and this is the grander picture. Remember the promise God made to our forefathers. Remember being led across the Jordan river to receive our land. Remember, you were not there when the earth was created in the days of darkness. Adonai gives us light. May we praise His name forever and ever. The last fleeting thoughts, the last corrections, the last acknowledgments send them all off for a later time. Listen to Adonai, your God, for Israel heard Him. Rest, no more work. Be merry and congregate, and recognize one another for who we are now, not who we could be. The heart of the king is like water in the hand of God. Do not delay. Take action, and you will always have strength if you rest on Shabbat.

I can breathe. I am awake. I am here. I know where I come from. I don't know much more. I think I know so much, yet I am proven differently. I am humbled and so honored to be here. Thank you, Adonai, my Lord, for this gift of life! Remember who you are, don't be carried away. Be who you need to be now. There is no better time.

There is a consistency to life outside of the constant change. Don't let that tell you consistency is how we are. We are made in the likeness of God. You are so much more than who you are right now. You could change right now. What has happened thus far? I've smoked a lot, but no more than I should've. I know what needs to be changed. No more buts. It either is, or it isn't. You know what it is you need to change, or sin rests at the door. It cannot be if God is with you.

Thank you, my Lord, for saving me and guiding me through the storm with strong winds. I see my destination, and I am so close. I am now aware, the picture is closer than before. You are my approach. It is you who allows me to see. I pray this is all for you, Adonai, for it is not us who are giving. It is you, my eternal father. My master, so kind and just. Blessed be He, Adonai/Elohim, my Master of masters, forever. Amen.

All is in the hand of God. Float through your day, work hard, work smart and spend your time wisely. We have selective action, the ability to choose an entirely different path at any given moment. Your decision can raise you to the heights of the heavens or the depth of the sea. Choose life, for that, is the whole of man. Remember who made you, like clay in its molder's palms. A God so awesome and kind, whose judgment is morality itself.

My Lord in heaven, whose awesome heavenly throne I serve. Redeem us, Elohim, for this perverse world can be saved only by your hand. I know you do not want to look, for our stench is putrid. Your nation assimilates. They rob, kill, rape, covet and commit abominable transgressions. May my plea for forgiveness be worthy, and may you remember me for my request. Blessed be my Lord Elohim, who provides for all of man!

I feel the change happening, pursuing and accepting bigger and better things. True fulfillment, the joy, and the light of Adonai. It is you who brought us up out of Egypt, and it is you whose judgment is always right. I pray for the opportunity to continue serving you for many more years and for it to continue beyond this life. That it is the purpose of man and that this gift of life is for us and no one else. Remember who you are, how special you are, and the history that brought us here. Let's blow the shofar and remember. I am processing it all a lot faster now. It takes the time that it takes. If you're out of the rut shorter, you've made progress. Congratulations, you've made it out of a ditch. Stay out of ditches. If God puts you there, God put you there for a reason. Correct the frame. Remember, your God loves you, but it is you who serve Him. This world openly defies and disobeys my Lord.

Please, our merciful father, do not destroy us, may the pleas of the righteous calm your anger. We can remember, and we will remember. Blessed be He who reigns over us all, Adonai/Elohim. May we praise your name eternally in this world and the next!

We are but clay in the molder's palms. He made you. He guides us all, and He shows unparalleled love. Blessed be Adonai, The God of the Jewish people, who gives us a choice to correct! May it be the will of your beloved children to correct themselves. May you bless me to be an example and have the blessings that only those whom God loves desire. I will continue to change in order to adapt to reality and serve courageously for Adonai, my Lord, the one and only God to which there is no power above.

My fear is in line with the truth. Truth is under your command, as is your command to us all. May my actions be upright and pure of heart. Guide my tongue and nullify the curses of my foes. May it fall upon them. I know your judgment is perfect. I will accept it and always question with faith. I am in your hands Adonai my Lord. I cannot deny my feelings, and you made me this way. I know there is a grand purpose ahead.

The path is foggy, but I still believe. You will save me from the hand of death, and the blade will not be unsheathed. Your light shines too bright to bear. I prostrate myself, crying on the floor with nothing to say except forgive me, my Lord. How can this be? So against the way of your Torah are we. Forgive us all, your mercy is endless, and your kindness is greater! Nothing soothes my soul more than your Torah. There's a slippery slope ahead, be ready. Prepare yourself at all times, and know the path ahead is not how it seems. You will not know. You cannot know. All is in the hand of God.

I am not normal. None of this is normal. Remove from your mind the issues of others, work on yourself and treat your neighbor like yourself. If you cared about yourself, you wouldn't think twice. It is always returned, for God's judgment is perfect. Thank you,

Adonai/Elohim, for allowing us to live, seek you, and receive love. It is nowhere else, not in true form with balance, but with crooked scales and mockers. Remove this perversion from our midst and redeem us all. Amen!

There is shame in this world, don't deny it. We all know it, so true to our own nature. Don't try to escape it. Recognize it and send him on his way. I have my own shames. I wish to cleanse myself of them and embrace a new man being reborn under the sun. How foolish I've been, so naive, so rude, a mocker, a scoffer, a jester. Please, my Lord Elohim, cleanse me, make me a more righteous man, a present one, and make me holy. I am no longer the boy I used to be, I am me now. Already more present, more attentive to your needs.

My Master in heaven, your kindness rules us all. We cower in fear of your anger. I wish only to please you and fulfill your requests. I know this is man's purpose, not some angel. Read Adonai's Torah of Moses, the Chumash, the Old Testament. Stop mixing up your terms and making others feel silly. The world is silly, you're living a joke. Grow up and make the necessary actions happen with speed. For you are no layman. You are a Jew, a Hebrew, an Israelite, an Ivri. Adonai's nation is a beloved one. Do not take your position lightly. We all need to take action. Start correcting shamelessly, anew, be holy, and reborn.

Adonai, bless us all to be cleansed fully and entirely. May we be redeemed before we anger you.

Amen!

The discomfort of being a child and the overbearing resilience of manhood. How could it be? The tide is weaker, and the waves are smaller. Yet the frame is much larger. As I float safely and freely as a child in the womb, knowing I have the protection of Adonai. It is through His will alone that we are allowed such magnificent experiences.

All has come from His hand, and they will continue too. Do not place your faith in anything other than God Himself, for there is nothing here that lasts. We all die, tomorrow may not come, and I can't live in fear of death. It is by God's hand that I have had the grace to be born, and it is by His hand I will go. I am a particle of sand engulfed in the sea. The contrast is very good. Thank you, my Lord Elohim, who reveals to us the miracles of His hand.

Who humbles us with His glory, whose very presence is the highest of heights. What more is worthy of speech other than for your praise? Your kindness pours over our heads like anointing oil, embracing our weak and futile lives, making us feel something real. May it be your will that we all pursue life and practice the search for your divine light, which is in all your creations. May it bring us all closer together and please You, Adonai/Elohim, my master and commander. Amen!

All of our feelings are valid. People are not good. You need to correct yourself in order to be good. Change needs to be accepted, or you will not get older. Men are too afraid to grow up, and women are too afraid to back down. A lesser regressed society. The sort of torturous rejection of God's gift of life. The struggle, the trauma, and the pain are all real. It's all part of the lovely life you have. It could be worse. Ask yourself, compared to what?

Unfortunately, people are not using their eyes, and they are not making their presence known.

Ashamed to be here?

What did you do? Take it all up with Adonai, He doesn't hate you. He created you, and He allows you to live. Love Him with all your heart and soul. Fear Him and no other. Observe and follow His commandments. Do not add or subtract. I will not go to the right or the left, and for this, I received my only peace. Serving my creator with all my heart and soul. All else is futile, don't deny it. It will only slow your integration, for you are to be loyal to your kind God.

Show Him what it means to you to be alive. To live a life that is so grand and beautiful, so perfect and just. Blessed be He Adonai Elohim, my Master whom no one is above, with all the blessings we can give for all of eternity. Amen! What does it mean to truly remember? What are you? Where do you come from? Adonai. He brought us to a land flowing with milk and honey, even after our betrayal at Mount Sinai.

He split the sea, and He saved us from our exile. He continues to save us all day long. It is at your disposal. Read the Torah of Moses. People are afraid to say his name, yet they wrong Adonai's holy name with smiles and glee. Moses was a man who led us to the land. Remember Adonai/Elohim, blow the horns, sweat, and be open to harmonizing with one another for the greater good. A service so beautiful it allows everyone to speak freely of who they are and the struggles they need to overcome.

Use the Torah as a means to understand one another. Truly listen, humble yourself and take time to prepare for your trial.

Yom Kippur is ten days away, and we need to remind ourselves, what for? Remember, we are all human, we are all struggling, and we cannot know the fate of another man. God will account for you, a much greater threat. Things are serious, life is serious. Use it to better yourself and create life.

The source of this miracle, this joy. One year ahead, alive and well, open to any and all of the change that is necessary, and all that I have learned is from your hand. I pray for us all to remove from our midst our own issues against the issues of a much greater good. Amen!

There is no other path to follow. The state of existence I live in is beyond decrepit. Only a year's worth of time, so much change, and yet so little recognition of it all. I am blessed by my creator, given a day of remembrance. What have I done this year? How have I served my creator, others, and myself? With Adonai at the forefront of my mind, all has been achieved, and all have been given correction.

Adonai is the judge, He cares about us, and we show Him we care with our actions. I pray we all take the necessary corrective action and recognize how much we all need to change. We can all be more blessed than our forefathers. God wants that for us, and so did they. There could be no better shoes to live in than your own. Thank Adonai, He gave this existence to us, He taught us how to act, and He makes us all flourish. I do not know what is ahead, and I do not know how much change can be achieved in a single day. I pray the proper recognitions are made. I pray the blessings shower us all, and we all rejoice in unity with Adonai, our Master in heaven. We heard you at Sinai. You spoke to us then. May we hear you again and be reminded with the sound of the shofar. Amen!

I remember I found what I was looking for. I died, and I was reborn. I am better, and I am stronger for it. My service to the only God, Adonai. It is He who does all. The Jews think Torah is a religion. They make a second day of holiday against your will so that they can have a day for themselves. Ungrateful, so little awareness. How could it be their fault? I open my eyes, preparing for the answer any day. "Am I not allowed to know, or am I not supposed to know?" This is the response. Stupid mindless thought so they can bow to the gods of others. Please save us from the evil within us all. If you believe in God, He will not forsake you.

Remember who you are, a beloved, a betrothed nation, a nation whom God loves. You can always lead with peace if another is willing to obey. We all obey the highest power of them all, the source of all light, a God so benevolent and kind, He creates us, and He will judge us. Plea for mercy and beg for forgiveness. The world is at stake. Do you really want it all to end? Is time not relevant anymore? How mixed up could we be? You have the Torah. Choose servitude to Adonai. He will give you this life and the next, and all will be blessed. Blessed be He Adonai, whose servitude heals us all. Amen!

Guilt. I'm not sure if what I did was right or wrong. I apply the Torah, I speak to you with all my being, and I await to hear you. Speak to me, my Lord, as I am too simple to solve. I was made to work, and work I do. I am made to guard, so I guard. It is not good to be alone, I know. I fall here often, unsatisfied without my other half. May she be righteous and beautiful of mind, body, and soul. I pray the same for myself.

Fully embodied masculine and fully embraced feminine. May it be so with all men and women. May that be real enough to set us straight. The crooked does not grow straight. Nothing is beyond God's hands. You can be saved, and you will be if you repent for your hearts and souls. This is not the garden, don't pretend you're not in exile.

The truth slices through. Let it break your silly beliefs and embody a new and better one. Older, much older. This time it's build your own ark. If you do not, this will not happen twice. The world is falling apart, people are decomposing, and gods preach religion. What I believe in is the only documented history on earth that is still valid. Praise Hashem/Elohim for His awesome mercy, kindness, and forgiveness. Please, my Lord, forgive us all. Amen!

So much unseen beauty. The sand sparkles like a diamond. The waters never stop. The boat in the ocean is like a fin in the sea. Seagulls are flying over the ocean. An ice cream salesman is working hard. We are all miracles, a miracle of God. Bless You, Adonai/Elohim, for creating us all in your likeness and bestowing in us life. How could it be? Your creations are so perfect, yet a life so distorted. Men and women who don't want to integrate. A marriage founded on the foundation of divorce. The whole purpose of life is thrown under ideologies such as school and a degree. It limits everyone's abilities and asks them to stably await a fight grand enough to call it quits. Vile women are trying to acquire negative power. To bring down their own homes and turn children against their fathers. It's torture. A fraud of availability. "You can look, but you can't touch." Naked women are walking the streets complaining about bad men. Put some clothes on, and you won't know so many bad men. A foolish culture built off of jokes. So silly it gets controlled by a handful of men who we know.

A purely Godless society, so unwilling to change for the good. We deserve God's judgment, it's the only source of truth we can use for our own judgments. Between the good, the bad, and the knowledge. It's a lot to sort out, and we do need God's help. Beg him for forgiveness, and He forgives. Blessed be He Adonai/Elohim, who guides us through all our days. Amen!

How vast can it all be? This is purely up to the individual. We are all God's children. He loves us all. How did we fall so far again? We couldn't be farther. The strain of living in such a dystopia and being unable to express it. True imprisonment. All in order to be a consumer. All this stuff is too good. This can't be worth settling human life over. Our birth rate is at an all-time low. Sons take their mothers and aunts out to salsa night. Lesbians play the music, and everyone calls abominable homosexuality pride.

We should all want to vomit the poison right out. "The problem is. It isn't that easy." Put away this silly idea of easy or planned. Life is constant work, and it comes in all forms and purposes. We are made unique with gender roles and guidance. We have the Torah, and all the nations do too. We are beyond blessed. How could one not obey fully? How good it could all be. Continue to wish good upon one another.

Forgive and ask for forgiveness. Our only hope is to open ourselves up to fully experience and take on the light of God. You are a priest amongst the nations. Adonai/Elohim will bless you more than your forefathers. The reward is grand, and God is perfect. Walk with perfection before Him. Bless your fellow with blessing to befall him, and Adonai will bless you in return tenfold.

Praise be He, who fulfills all blessings. Amen!

What is it that I'm not getting? Adonai, you are my ruler. It is you who I turn my attention to. I pray I am not a fool. You have talked to me, my Lord. I have seen it. I truly believe I'm on the right path. I know you are watching over me always, nurturing me along the grand journey of life. I know the things to come are much better. I am willing to leave it all behind. This back-and-forth is really too much.

The path ahead is one best made without unnecessary vows. Forgive me, Adonai, my Lord, for my loud mouth and lack of understanding. I don't believe I've ever been a bad guy. Everywhere in my life it was always assumed that I've had experiences I did not have far before I was having those experiences. All the moments of my life were raw and filtered. It's the only way you will stay clean. Do not dirty your soul for any price. The soul is not a park to roam around in. Matters of the soul are grand. It is your higher self-bettering you every day if you think a little harder. We all absolutely need forgiveness. It needs to stem from kindness and truth. Your intentions matter. I'm pretty sure all of it does. How good can you be? Know that the blessing outweighs the hardship. Don't bury yourself before the blessing has room to grow. "The early rains and the late rains." It will rain all day. Blessed be He Adonai/Elohim, who blesses and forgives. Amen!

The final analysis is we are all naked in front of God. If you have no shame with others, what is there to correct? We are not here to dither around and dance in the shadows. We are elevated creatures in the divine likeness. What we can do for this world and others is truly cosmic. The grand enough change to accept it all.

What more can we do? Adonai, my Lord, I am ashamed. I can be better, much better, and I am lazy. Please heal me with your light, changing the course of the soul to follow God and not evil. The evil in this world lurks around, pretending it's a friend. Adonai protects us from evildoers who seek to do us harm. Give us the awareness to accept ourselves fully and totally, to better ourselves and one another. If you yourself are not guilty of anything, don't waste your time begging for forgiveness. You are forgiven. Pray for your lost brothers and sisters, husbands, wives, sons, and daughters.

Do not let your parents define you. Use moral and just judgment for all men and women alike. Honor your father and mother, and you will live a long life. All your deeds are recognized, Adonai sees all, pray to Him fully and repent sorrowfully in hopes of saving your life and having it forgiven. You will start to witness plentiful blessings in your life. Reward like you've never heard of and most definitely never seen. Your individuality is everything. Express it till your last breath. Praise the mighty Lord in heaven, Adonai/Elohim. Amen!

This was the end of my journal. When I had finished writing the prayer, I went right into Yom Kippur, God's holy day of atonement, cleansing, and forgiveness.

Chapter 7

During a period while writing this book, I was in a relationship with the second girl. I wrote her our vows. It was for her. It is now gone, but I did write a conclusion. I believe it's worth sharing for all men who have to bear the burning heat of a contentious woman. Adam was cursed because he listened to his wife. Correcting the original sin can never be the wrong decision. Both these women were only in my life to improve me, and they have. Here it is.

"I made a mistake, and my judgment was off. I accept it, I know the journey was necessary, and nothing will ever be the same. A true love story, so few of those left. I have counted my blessings, and I know the next woman is my truest love. The most developed, beautiful, and righteous woman I will ever know. I pray that other women see that marriage is to save themselves from this pitiful excuse of a life. If you want something good, be good at it, and it will come to you. There is so little I know. Yet I have so much to share. I am speaking with God. He knows me, and He sends me everything. My strength lies there. I pray I don't fall ever again. May only blessings appear in my lifetime here and in the next. Praise Adonai /Elohim for creating us, for giving us life, and for bestowing us with His Torah. Amen!"

15945107R00049